# The Split History of

# WESTWARD EXPANSION
## IN THE UNITED STATES

# SETTLERS' PERSPECTIVE

BY NELL MUSOLF

CONTENT CONSULTANT:
Malcolm Rohrbough
Professor of History Emeritus
University of Iowa

COMPASS POINT BOOKS
a capstone imprint

## ABOUT THE AUTHOR:

Nell Musolf is a freelance writer in Mankato, Minnesota. She writes fiction and nonfiction. Her work has appeared in several magazines and newspapers. Musolf holds a bachelor's degree in psychology from Northeastern Illinois University.

## SOURCE NOTES:

**American Indian Perspective**

Page 5, line 8: PBS New Perspectives on the West—Chief Joseph. 13 April 2012. www.pbs.org/weta/thewest/people/a_c/chiefjoseph.htm

Page 15, line 3: Thomas B. Underwood. *Cherokee Legends and the Trail of Tears*. Knoxville, Tenn.: Cherokee Publications, 1956, p. 27.

Page 20, line 9: Joyce Appleby, et al. *The American Journey*. Columbus, Ohio: McGraw-Hill, 2012, p. 398.

Page 28, line 8: Digital History—Native American Voices. 13 April 2012. www.digitalhistory.uh.edu/native_voices/voices_display.cfm?id=88

Page 29, sidebar, line 12: Tom Pendergast and Sara Pendergast. *Westward Expansion Almanac*. Detroit: U X L, 2000, p. 190.

**Settlers' Perspective**

Page 10, line 11: *The American Journey*, p. 363.

Page 14, line 5: Lillian Schissel. *Women's Diaries of the Westward Journey*. New York: Schocken Books, 1982, p. 36.

Page 19, line 5: Ibid., p. 122.

Page 24, line 8: *The American Journey*, p. 556.

# Table of Contents

# THE BEGINNING

*I*n April 1853 the Knight family—Joel, Amelia, and their seven children—left Monroe County, Iowa, in a covered wagon. Their plan was to travel west to Oregon Territory. During the next five months, they endured sickness, storms, and the loss of many of their livestock. They reached Oregon in mid-September, where Amelia Knight gave birth in the covered wagon to her eighth child. A few days later the Knight family crossed the Columbia River into Washington Territory, where they traded two yoke of oxen for a piece of land and a small log cabin.

*Settlers journeyed west by wagon and on horseback.*

The Knight family wasn't unique. In the 1800s thousands of Americans traveled from their homes in the East and Midwest to new lives in the West—a time known as westward expansion.

In the years since 1492, when Christopher Columbus made his first journey to the New World, England, France, Spain, and the Netherlands had all claimed land on the continent and tried to start colonies. In April 1607 the Virginia Company of London, England, established the first permanent English settlement in North America, Jamestown Colony. Jamestown was located about 60 miles (97 kilometers) from the Chesapeake Bay in what is now Virginia.

*Colonists landed at Jamestown Island May 14, 1607.*

In America the European settlers would be able to own land, a goal most knew they'd never be able to achieve in Europe. But the settlers who made the difficult journey across the ocean faced hard times in their new country, including starvation, American Indian attacks, and disease. Of the 104 settlers who arrived in Jamestown in spring 1607, fewer than 40 were alive by the winter of 1608. But the colonists persevered, and more settlers arrived, including those who established Plymouth Colony in what is now Massachusetts in 1620.

The settlers built towns and villages along the east coast of North America next to the Atlantic Ocean, an important passageway for ships and also a place where the settlers could harvest seafood to supplement their diet. Virginia became a British royal colony in 1624, and by 1670 Britain had 12 colonies in what is now the eastern United States. Georgia, the 13th original colony, was established in 1733.

By the 1700s the American colonies included three separate regions: New England, the Middle Atlantic colonies, and the South. But although the regions were distinct from one another, they united to fight the British for their independence in the Revolutionary War (1775–1783). The colonies won their freedom from British rule and were now the United States of America.

As the population of the eastern United States grew, the government wanted people to settle the West. Congress assisted this goal by enacting the Land Ordinance of 1785. This law created a uniform system in which land was divided into ships of 36 square miles (93 square km). Each township was divided into 36 sections,

*The American victory at Yorktown, Virginia, marked the last major battle of the Revolutionary War.*

which were made up of 640 acres (259 hectares). In 1787 Congress enacted the Northwest Ordinance. This act established government and laws in an area north of the Ohio River and east of the Mississippi River—now the states of Michigan, Wisconsin, Ohio, Indiana, and Illinois. The U.S. government sold land to anyone who could afford it, raising money for the government and helping settlers move west at the same time. Many people took them up on the offer, which began a large westward migration.

## LOUISIANA PURCHASE

In 1803 the United States increased in size considerably. That was the year the United States bought 828,000 square miles (2.1 million square km) of land from France. The land cost $15 million and covered a huge section west of the Mississippi River. After the Louisiana Purchase, the size of the United States doubled.

President Thomas Jefferson hired Meriwether Lewis and William Clark to explore the newly acquired lands. He was especially interested in having Lewis and Clark look for a river that extended west from the Mississippi River to the Pacific Ocean. A river route would make it easier to move goods from the East to the West. The explorers left on their journey from St. Louis, Missouri, in 1804.

The Lewis and Clark expedition lasted two years. When the explorers returned in 1806, they told Jefferson that while they didn't find a river that ran all the way to the ocean, they did

*Meriwether Lewis*

*William Clark*

discover a land filled with animals that could be trapped, thick forests, huge mountain ranges, and thousands of acres of land—plus a number of American Indian groups who were living there. Over the next several years, settlers flocked to the area. By 1840 the states of Louisiana, Arkansas, and Missouri had been formed from some of the land in the Louisiana Purchase.

## MANIFEST DESTINY

In the 1840s a belief called Manifest Destiny began to gain popularity among Americans. It was the belief that God wanted Americans to live across the entire continent, from the Atlantic Ocean to the Pacific. Newspaper editor John O'Sullivan coined the term in 1845. He wrote that it was the United States' "Manifest Destiny to overspread and to possess the whole of the continent which Providence has given us."

O'Sullivan summed up what many Americans had believed for a long time—that they had the right to live wherever they wanted and that it was their destiny to take any land they wanted. They believed that was what God wanted them to do. These Americans didn't think that they were taking land from the American Indians. Instead they would be settling the land and improving it both for themselves and for future generations. They would also be spreading Christianity at the same time.

In 1845 the United States tested the theory of Manifest Destiny by annexing the Republic of Texas. It had been part of Mexico until declaring independence in 1836. The United States went to war with Mexico over disputes about Texas' borders. The U.S. won the two-year Mexican War in 1848. Under the Treaty of Guadalupe Hidalgo, Mexico gave what is now the states of California, New Mexico, and Arizona to the U.S. in return for $15 million.

The land that opened up to settlers during the westward expansion was huge. It extended from the Appalachian Mountains to the Pacific Ocean. It spread from the Mexican border in the south to the Canadian border in the north. For the settlers who were moving from eastern cities, the frontier sounded like a dream. A dream that was about to come true.

*The U.S. gained about 525,000 square miles (1.4 million square km) of territory after winning the Mexican War.*

# SETTLING THE WEST

The U.S. government encouraged people to move west, especially families. The government believed that families would settle land quickly and make it a safe, desirable place to live. With settlers farming the land, establishing towns, and building churches, the West would soon become a prosperous place, and the entire U.S. would benefit.

In 1838 the government founded the Corps of Topographical Engineers. The group would survey western lands and decide what land was best for settlements. It would map the region to give settlers a better idea of what the West looked like. The maps would help people plan their trips westward.

*People began moving west in large numbers around 1840.*

The government helped people settle the West by selling tracts of land to any settler who could afford it. By the 1830s the government was selling 40-acre (16-hectare) lots of land for $1.25 an acre. At that price many families could afford to buy land.

## WAGON TRAINS

Between 1840 and 1870, about half a million settlers headed west. Many traveled on the Santa Fe Trail or the Oregon Trail. The 900-mile (1,448-km) Santa Fe Trail began in Missouri and ended in New Mexico territory. The Oregon Trail also started in Missouri and spanned 2,170 miles (3,492 km) to the Pacific Northwest.

It wasn't easy to move out west. Settlers had to leave friends and family behind, knowing that they might never see them again. Once

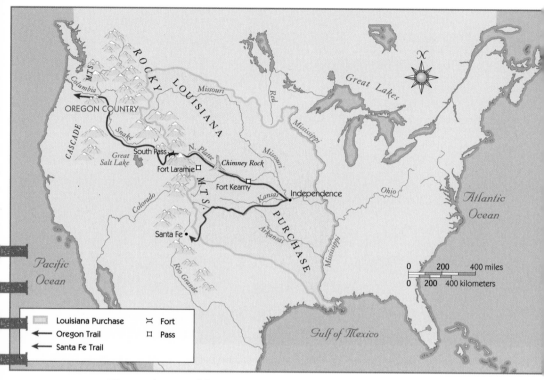

*Most settlers traveled west on either the Oregon Trail or the Santa Fe Trail.*

on the trail, they were forced to rely completely on themselves and their traveling companions. As a result, people who wanted to move west were usually independent and used to hard work. Thirteen-year-old Martha Morrison headed to Oregon with her family in 1844: "We did not know the dangers we were going through. The idea of my Father was to get to the coast; no other place suited him, and he went right ahead until he got there …"

People traveled west in covered wagons. Oxen were stronger than horses, so they usually pulled the wagons. The covered wagons were not very big—a little larger than an SUV or minivan—and couldn't hold more than 2,000 pounds (907 kilograms). People could bring only the things they needed for survival. Some people tried to take large pieces of furniture with them when they moved. More often than not, those big pieces of furniture ended up on the side of the trail when their owners decided not to haul them any farther. The settlers quickly learned that when the trails got rough, the extra weight of anything large made traveling much harder.

Some families made the trip alone, but most traveled in groups. Wagon trains usually included 20 to 40 wagons, but some had more than 100. Wagon trains typically traveled between eight and 20 miles (13 and 32 km) each day. If rainy weather turned the trail to mud, they didn't travel as far. But if the weather was good and everyone in the group was well, they traveled as far as they could. Settlers

## THE DONNER PARTY

Perhaps the most tragic story of the Oregon Trail is that of the Donner Party. The Donner Party was made up of about 200 men, women, and children who left Independence, Missouri, in May 1846 to travel on the Oregon Trail to California.

Bad weather plagued the travelers from the beginning, first with heavy rains and then snow in the mountains. In Wyoming 87 members of the party made a fatal mistake by leaving the Oregon Trail to take what they believed would be a shortcut. By early November the party was trapped in the Sierra Nevada mountains. Starving, some most likely resorted to cannibalism, eating the flesh of their dead companions to survive. Just 47 of the original 87 members of the group lived to reach California.

left Independence, Missouri—called the "jumping-off point" for the Oregon Trail—in May so they could cross the Rocky Mountains before the winter snows closed the passes.

## LIFE AND DEATH ON THE TRAILS

When settlers were done traveling for the day, there were chores to be done before they could rest. They had to find water, care for their animals, set up camp, and prepare meals. They supplemented the food they brought with them with game they hunted or fish caught in streams, lakes, and rivers.

*Settlers risked death from drowning as they crossed rivers.*

Many settlers worried about the American Indians they might meet along the way. But attacks from Indians were rare. Most deaths on the trail were caused by disease, accidental gunshot wounds, or drowning. When settlers reached rivers, there were no bridges. Figuring out how to cross rivers without drowning or losing everything they owned was a constant challenge.

If the settlers got sick or hurt, there were often no doctors available. Illnesses were common and often transmitted from one group of settlers to another. Many settlers became sick with pneumonia, whooping cough, measles, or smallpox. They often died before reaching their final destination. Graves of men, women, and children dotted the trails.

Cholera was the deadliest disease. The infection of the intestines causes fever, chills, vomiting, and diarrhea. Settlers who came down with cholera often died within days. In the late 1840s a severe outbreak of cholera swept through groups of settlers. Of about 350,000 people who set out on the Oregon Trail between 1840 and 1860, it is estimated that about 20,000 died from disease, never seeing their new homes.

For the settlers, moving onto land where American Indians already lived could be a dangerous proposition. As the settlers came into their territories, the American Indians were forced by the government to move off the land to less desirable places. Conflicts were bound to happen.

American Indians sometimes burned the settlers' houses, barns, and crops. They stole horses and livestock. Sometimes they killed settlers.

## ARMY INVOLVEMENT

As settlers moved west, the U.S. Army moved along with them. The army built a number of forts in the West—some permanent, but many others temporary settlements that were eventually abandoned. At first the army's purpose in the West was to keep peace among warring American Indian tribes and to keep white settlers from disregarding treaties and taking over Indian lands. As more settlers came west, though, clashes between Indians and

*Violence between settlers and American Indians increased as more settlers migrated west.*

settlers increased. The army's role then became to protect
the settlers from Indian attacks.

In the summer of 1854, Mary Perry Frost and her party faced
unfriendly Indians in what is now Idaho.

"We had traveled perhaps an hour … Then Indians … came up
squarely in front of our train and stopped the teams, but appeared
friendly, shaking hands and asking for whiskey; upon being told that
we had none they began to talk of trading with the men, and while
my father was talking of trading a pistol for a pony, they opened fire
on us, shooting my father, my uncle and my father's teamster."

## THE HOMESTEAD ACT OF 1862

The Homestead Act of 1862 gave, for a $10 filing
fee, 160 acres (65 hectares) of land to any settler
who was willing to live on the land for five
years. The act encouraged thousands of people to
move to the Great Plains, the land between the
Mississippi River and the Rocky Mountains. Small
farmers claimed about 80 million acres (32 million
hectares) through the act.

# CONNECTING THE EAST AND WEST

Western settlers needed supplies such as cloth, tools, and nails, as well as food staples of flour, coffee, and sugar. Transportation systems were built to get needed goods to the settlers.

Canals connected natural waterways, making it much easier for goods to be carried from one part of the country to another. The Erie Canal was built to connect Lake Erie with the Hudson River in New York. After it was finished in 1825, it was possible to ship goods across New York much more quickly. Instead of taking weeks for a shipment of goods to arrive, it only took eight days. The finished canal was 363 miles (584 km) long.

*The Erie Canal, completed in 1825, allowed goods to be shipped between the Atlantic Ocean and the Great Lakes.*

In 1848 the 96-mile (155-km) Illinois and Michigan Canal was completed on the Chicago and Illinois rivers. The canal created a water route from the Mississippi River to the Great Lakes, allowing shipment of bulky items such as stone, lumber, and grain.

Many areas of the West didn't have strong river systems that would support canals. Canals also froze during cold winters and needed continual maintenance to keep operating. Another form of fast transportation was needed for the West. That system was the Iron Horse—the railroad.

Before settlers began to move west, railroads already crisscrossed much of the East, connecting small towns to big cities. Huge steam engines pulled train cars loaded with freight and other cars filled with passengers. President Abraham Lincoln wanted a train line that would run across the country to California. In 1863 construction began on the transcontinental railroad.

## A MASSIVE UNDERTAKING

In Omaha, Nebraska, the Union Pacific Company began work on a transcontinental railroad. The Central Pacific Company began doing the same thing in Sacramento, California. The two companies began laying track with the plan that they would eventually meet in the middle and become one railroad line.

*The transcontinental railroad's Promontory Trestle in Utah spanned 450 feet (137 meters)*

Building the large railroad was a huge undertaking. It would have to go over grassy prairies and through steep mountain passes. Bridges had to be built over rivers and gorges. Thousands of workers were needed to clear the land, tunnel through the mountains, and lay track.

In the West 12,000 Chinese workers helped blast passages through the Sierra Nevada for the Central Pacific. The Chinese gained reputations as hard workers, making them desirable employees. In the Nebraska Territory, 10,000 men worked on the railroad for the Union Pacific, including Irish immigrants and African-Americans.

Workers faced harsh blizzards, windstorms, the blazing sun, and the bitter cold. Accidents and illnesses claimed many lives.

## MORMON SETTLEMENT

Mormons belong to the Church of Jesus Christ of Latter-day Saints. Joseph Smith founded the church in New York in 1830. Many people didn't care for the church's ideas, so Mormons moved to Ohio, Missouri, and then Illinois, searching for a place to practice their religion. After Smith was murdered in 1844, Mormon leader Brigham Young moved the center of the church farther west, finally settling in 1847 near the Great Salt Lake in present-day Utah. By 1849 about 5,000 Mormons lived in Utah, building the town of Salt Lake City, which is the center of the Mormon Church.

The workers also worried about attacks by American Indians. The Indians didn't want to see the railroad completed, since it was sure to bring more settlers.

But the work continued, and the transcontinental railroad was finished in 1869, transforming the U.S. in the process. At a May 10 ceremony in Promontory, Utah, silver, gold, and iron spikes were used to complete the track. A telegraph message spread the news across the country. "The last rail is laid ... the Pacific Railroad is completed." All over the country, people began to celebrate as soon as they heard the news. It was now possible to travel from one American coast to the other on the railroad. Wagon travel soon became a thing of the past. Anyone who could afford the price of a railroad ticket could go west.

*Officials of the Central Pacific and Union Pacific Railroad, along with other dignitaries, attended the Golden Spike ceremony May 10, 1869.*

# The Pony Express

Founded in 1860, the Pony Express was a system that delivered mail across the country in 10 days. The route of the Pony Express was almost 2,000 miles (3,219 km) long. Pony Express riders, mostly teenage boys who were able to handle the physical challenges of the job, rode horses as fast as they could. Riding the horses so fast wore them out, so new horses were needed constantly. Riders got fresh horses every 10 to 20 miles (16 to 32 km) at Pony Express stations. The Pony Express lasted only 19 months. In 1861 the transcontinental telegraph system, which sent messages across the country in minutes, ended the need for the fast riders of the Pony Express.

# FROM SEA TO SHINING SEA

In 1890 the superintendent of the U.S. Census Bureau, Robert Porter, announced that there was no longer an identifiable frontier line. The West had been settled. Cities, towns, and villages could be found across the country. Each region was slightly different, but all of them added up to make a rich tapestry that was the United States of America.

The settlers who moved west were part of an amazing journey. They had left the settled East and started new lives in a new place. People who had never owned anything now owned the land they lived on.

*The Semler family of Custer County, Nebraska, were among the settlers who built houses and farms in the West.*

Most of the land in the western interior of the United States is considered semi-arid. It receives an average of less than 20 inches (51 centimeters) of rain each year. In order to grow crops, irrigation is often needed. Farmers had to dig deep wells and build windmills to pump water to the crops.

Not everyone who settled the West made smart choices about the land. There was so much land available that people sometimes acted as if there was a never-ending supply of trees, fresh water, and fertile soil. Some settlers were wasteful when it came to protecting their new land. Some cut down too many trees or ruined the soil by overplanting. Still others were careless when they mined such metals as gold, copper, and silver, wasting

# THE GOLD RUSH

Not everyone went west to build farms and towns. On January 24, 1848, James Marshall discovered gold near Sutter's Mill, California. That discovery led to "gold fever." People from all over the country rushed to California to pan for gold. By the end of the year, 8,000 men searching for gold had moved to California, which became a state in 1850. By 1851 that number reached 100,000.

The Gold Rush lasted only a few years, peaking in 1853. But it forever changed the West. California's population continued to grow, reaching 380,000 in 1860.

*By 1890 Stockton, California, was a prosperous town.*

minerals in the process and polluting the surrounding land and streams for generations to come.

Most settlers did everything they could to make their new homeland a good place to live. They worked to build productive farms and ranches that were able to support their families. The long, difficult trip west made them grateful for their new lives, and they wanted to make the most of it.

The United States had become a nation that stretched from one ocean to another. Instead of many regions sharing a continent, the U.S. became one united land. Settling the frontier gave Americans a sense of pride. For the people who made it to the new land in the West, their dream had come true.

# INDEX

COMPASS POINT BOOKS
a capstone imprint

CONTENT CONSULTANT
Malcolm Rohrbough
Professor of History Emeritus
University of Iowa

BY NELL MUSOLF

# AMERICAN INDIAN PERSPECTIVE

---

# WESTWARD EXPANSION
# IN THE UNITED STATES

The Split History of

A PERSPECTIVES FLIP BOOK

Compass Point Books
1710 Roe Crest Drive
North Mankato, Minnesota 56003
www.capstonepub.com

Library of Congress Cataloging-in-Publication Data
Musolf, Nell.
  The split history of westward expansion in the United States : a perspectives flip book /
by Nell Musolf.
     p. cm. —  (Perspectives flip book)
  Includes bibliographical references and index.
  Summary: "Describes the opposing viewpoints of the American Indians and settlers during the
Westward Expansion"— Provided by publisher.
  ISBN 978-0-7565-4571-0 (library binding)
  ISBN 978-0-7565-4596-3 (paperback)
  ISBN 978-0-7565-4631-1 (ebook PDF)
  1.  United States— Territorial expansion— Juvenile literature. 2.  Frontier and pioneer
life— West (U.S.)— Juvenile literature. 3.  Indians of North America— West (U.S.)
— History— Juvenile literature.  I. Title.
  E179.5.M88 2013
  978'.01— dc23                                                                 2012004747

EDITOR
ANGIE KAELBERER

LIBRARY CONSULTANT
KATHLEEN BAXTER

DESIGNER
ASHLEE SUKER

PRODUCTION SPECIALIST
MICHELLE BIEDSCHEID

MEDIA RESEARCHER
ERIC GOHL

## IMAGE CREDITS

**American Indian Perspective:** Alamy: INTERFOTO, cover (top), Lordprice Collection, 10, North
Wind Picture Archives, cover (bottom), 20; Corbis: Bettmann, 9; Library of Congress: 5, 13, 17, 21,
24, 25, 27, 28; National Parks Service: Colonial National Historical Park, 7; Newscom: akg-images,
19; Courtesy Scotts Bluff National Monument: 11; Wikimedia: Public Domain, 23

**Settlers' Perspective:** Alamy: INTERFOTO, cover (bottom), North Wind Picture Archives, cover
(top), 16; Corbis: Bettmann, 6, 21, National Geographic Society/W. Langdon Kihn, 18; Getty
Images: MPI, 13; iStockphotos: Duncan Walker, 28; Library of Congress: 5, 27, 29; Newscom:
World History Archive, 24; Courtesy Scotts Bluff National Monument: 25; Wikimedia: Public
Domain, 9 (all), 22; Wikipedia: Public Domain, 7, 11

Printed in the United States of America in Stevens Point, Wisconsin.
042012      006678WZF12

# Table of Contents

## SHARED RESOURCES

# A THREATENED WAY OF LIFE

Chief Him-mah-too-yah-lat-kekt, also known as Chief Joseph, was the well-respected leader of a band of Nez Percé living in the Wallowa Valley of Oregon. When gold was discovered in 1877, the U.S. government took nearly 6 million acres (2.4 million hectares) from the band's reservation and tried to force them to a smaller reservation in what is now Idaho. Angered over the loss of their land, about 20 young men of the tribe attacked and killed several white settlers. The U.S. Army was charged with finding and punishing the warriors.

*Chief Joseph led his people from 1871 until his death in 1904.*

Chief Joseph opposed war but knew he had to defend his people. During the next three months, the chief and his band led the army on a 1,400-mile (2,253-kilometer) chase into what is now Montana, fighting four major battles along the way despite being outnumbered about 10 to one. But they couldn't run forever. When Chief Joseph surrendered October 5, 1877, he sadly spoke these words:

"I am tired of fighting … It is cold, and we have no blankets. The little children are freezing to death. My people, some of them, have run away to the hills, and have no blankets, no food. No one knows where they are—perhaps freezing to death. I want to have time to look for my children, and see how many of them I can find. Maybe I

shall find them among the dead. Hear me, my chiefs! I am tired. My heart is sick and sad. From where the sun now stands I will fight no more forever."

American Indians lived in North America for thousands of years before European settlers arrived. The Indian people lived in many separate tribal groups across the continent. Each of the more than 600 tribes had its own language, culture, and way of life.

Some of the tribes stayed in one area. Others moved from place to place, following buffalo herds or changes in the weather. American Indian tribes shared a deep respect for nature. The majority of them believed that land was something no one could own, not themselves or the settlers. They believed that land could be used for a while, but must be preserved to be passed on to the next generation. Most also believed people were only a small part of nature and had a moral and spiritual obligation to give back whatever they took.

## NEW INHABITANTS

When European settlers came to North America, many of them in the 1600s, Indians were curious about the new people who had moved to their land. The American Indians helped the settlers by guiding them through the area and giving them assistance as they set up their farms, sharing what they knew about native plants and animals. The Indians also warned the newcomers about dangerous winter weather. In 1607 Chief Wahunsenacawh, known to the settlers as Chief Powhatan, supplied food to hungry settlers in the

*Powhatan people traded food to the Jamestown colonists.*

colony of Jamestown, in what is now Virginia. In 1621 a Patuxet
Indian named Tisquantam, also called Squanto, helped the settlers
of Plymouth Colony survive by teaching them native methods of
fishing and farming.

But as more and more settlers came to North America through
the 1700s, the majority of American Indians grew increasingly
unhappy. The settlers were moving onto land where the American
Indians already lived. The Indians didn't like seeing the land
that they hunted, fished, and lived on being taken over. Their
unhappiness sometimes led to attacks on the settlers. The Indians
believed that if they fought the settlers, the settlers would be
frightened into leaving.

The settlers didn't go away. Instead, more immigrants moved to the United States every year. As the eastern United States became settled, the government wanted to expand its boundaries. But if the country was going to grow, it needed more land, so the government looked west.

In 1803 the United States doubled in size with the purchase of vast tracts of land from France, called the Louisiana Purchase. The Louisiana Purchase gave the United States an additional 828,000 square miles (2.1 million square km) of land.

President Thomas Jefferson chose the exploration team of Meriwether Lewis and William Clark to go into the new territory to survey the land. The explorers' reports on their journey into the Northwest encouraged more settlers to move west. These western lands weren't empty, however. American Indians had made them their homes for centuries.

## BROKEN TREATIES

In order to get the land in the west, the government began to negotiate with American Indians. Government leaders traded such things as guns, horses, and clothing with the Indians in exchange for the land. The Indians signed treaties that said they were giving their land to the United States. The treaties also said that the tribes would have to move off their land to reservations—land the government had chosen specifically for them. But reservations were usually on poor land where no one else wanted to live and were almost always much smaller than the Indians had been told they would be.

# SACAGAWEA

Sacagawea, a young Shoshone woman, helped Lewis and Clark explore the Pacific Northwest.

Sacagawea was married to Frenchman Toussaint Charbonneau, who was hired as an interpreter by Lewis and Clark. A pregnant Sacagawea was allowed to come on the expedition as a Shoshone interpreter. Her son, Jean Baptiste, was born on the trail. No one knows what happened to Sacagawea after the expedition ended. But most historians believe she died in 1812 in South Dakota.

*Sacagawea (center) served as an interpreter for Lewis and Clark.*

As the 1800s continued, more treaties were signed between the U.S. government and the American Indians. With every treaty, the American Indians lost additional land and were forced to relocate.

As the settlers traveled west, the routes they took were the ones that best suited their needs. All too often the treaties made with the

*American Indians uneasily watched the settlers move onto their land.*

Indians were ignored, and the settlers crushed grasses and scared away game. This upset the Indians, but since there was still plenty of land available, they often chose not to fight.

Some Indians were hopeful that they would be able to get along with the settlers. But the majority of American Indians weren't as optimistic. They felt cheated by the U.S. government and angry over how they were treated.

It seemed clear to the American Indians that westward expansion was going to mean a huge change in the way they lived their lives. It was also clear that there wasn't much that they could do about it.

# Fur Trappers and American Indians

White fur trappers came to the West beginning in the 1640s. The trappers hunted and trapped animals for their furs, which they sold in the East. Trappers never stayed long in one place. They moved around the countryside, always on the lookout for good places to trap.

The trappers were the first white settlers most American Indians had ever seen. As the trappers and Indians got to know each other, they got along well. Many American Indians helped trappers by showing them around the unfamiliar land and by acting as their guides.

Fur trappers and American Indians shared an annual event every summer near the borders of present-day Idaho, Wyoming, and Utah. Called the Rendezvous, it was a combination of games, gambling, and storytelling that lasted for several days.

*Trappers and American Indians gathered each year for the Rendezvous.*

# TROUBLES IN THE EAST AND WEST

The U.S. government continued its push westward. The goal was for the West to be settled by families who would turn the land into profitable farms, ranches, and towns. Government leaders wanted the western half of the United States to resemble the East.

The American Indians watched the changes that were happening around them in dismay. They knew their way of life would never be the same.

The Cherokee, the Chickasaw, the Creek, the Choctaw, and the Seminole tribes lived in the southeastern United States. They were known as the Five Civilized Tribes because they had assimilated in

*Sequoyah developed a written alphabet for the Cherokee language.*

many ways with their white neighbors, including becoming farmers, establishing towns, and learning to read and write. In general, they got along well with the settlers, but that began to change as the demand for land grew.

In 1830 President Andrew Jackson signed the Indian Removal Act, which allowed the federal government to relocate American Indians who lived east of the Mississippi River, including the Five Civilized Tribes. Tribes that signed the government treaties would have to move west of the Mississippi River to an area called Indian Territory. Indian Territory was located in present-day Oklahoma, more than 1,000 miles (1,600 km) from the tribal homelands.

Under the terms of the Indian Removal Act, the tribes were supposed to be allowed to make their own decisions about relocating. The Choctaw and Chickasaw chose to sign treaties and move. The Creek signed a treaty that would allow them to stay in Alabama while giving up a large part of their land to settlers. The Creek soon lost their land to the settlers, and in 1836 they were forced to move west.

While a few members of the Seminole and Cherokee tribes had signed removal treaties, most tribe members wanted to stay and declared the treaties invalid. The Seminoles went to war three times in an effort to keep their land in Florida, but by the early 1840s most had left and moved west.

## TRAIL OF TEARS

The Cherokee decided to use the legal system to try to keep their land. In 1831 the tribe sued the state of Georgia. The state had passed a law in 1830 outlawing whites from living on Indian land, which was aimed at white missionaries who were helping the Cherokee. The case went to the U.S. Supreme Court, which ruled in the Cherokees' favor. But President Andrew Jackson would not enforce the ruling. In 1836 the government gave the Cherokee two years to pack up and leave. Most refused.

In 1838 the government sent in 7,000 soldiers to force the Cherokee to leave. About 15,000 men, women, and children began walking 1,200 miles (1,931 km) from Georgia to Indian Territory. Along the way about 4,000 died of exposure, starvation, and disease.

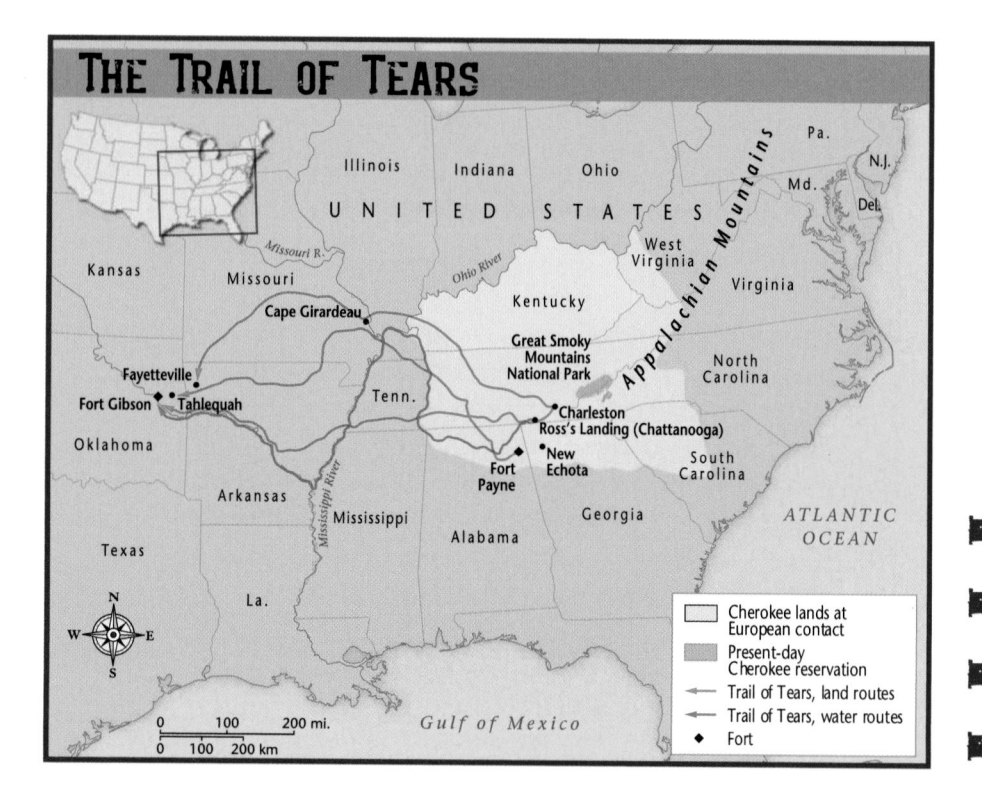

## THE TRAIL OF TEARS

Cherokees still remember it as the Trail of Tears. Recalling the long
walk many years later, former Army Private John G. Burnett wrote:

"Murder is murder and somebody must answer, somebody must
explain the streams of blood that flowed in the Indian country in
the summer of 1838. Somebody must explain the four thousand
silent graves that mark the trail of the Cherokees to their exile.
I wish I could forget it all, but the picture of six-hundred and
forty-five wagons lumbering over the frozen ground with their
Cargo of suffering humanity still lingers in my memory."

American Indians who were forced to move west of the
Mississippi River likely hoped that they would be allowed to live
in peace. But that wasn't to be.

## DEADLY DISEASES

American Indians had good reason to fear the settlers, who brought deadly diseases with them as they moved west. Since they had never been exposed to the germs that caused measles, cholera, and smallpox, the Indians didn't have any immunity. An outbreak of smallpox in 1837 almost wiped out the Mandan tribe of North Dakota. The Lakota and the Cheyenne tribes of the Great Plains suffered many deaths from an outbreak of cholera in the late 1840s.

Many Americans supported the idea of Manifest Destiny—the belief that white Americans were meant to own all of the land from coast to coast because that is what God wanted. They saw nothing wrong with taking any land they wanted, even land occupied by American Indians. As the white population slowly inched its way west, Indians had to either fight to hold onto their land or leave.

Fighting among Indian tribes over territory or other issues was not unusual. The lack of unity among the tribes weakened the Indians as they fought westward expansion. Another advantage for the Army and the settlers was that almost everyone spoke the same language—English—while the Indians didn't. With various tribes living all over the country, gaps in communication made coming together as a united force against the settlers and the Army almost impossible.

Their fighting methods also hampered the American Indian tribes. Depending on the tribe, Indian warriors were skilled fighters with knives, lances, and bows and arrows. The Indians believed that the closer you were to your enemy, the greater and more honorable the victory. The soldiers and the settlers fought back with guns, which were deadly at long distances.

When Indians did choose to fight, they often fought alone or in small groups. They attacked settlers on their way west or single families on their homesteads, stealing horses and burning down houses, farms, and crops. Fear of Indian attacks—and of Indians—grew among the settlers.

*American Indians preferred to fight at close range.*

# RAILROADS, BUFFALO, AND GOLD

**W**hen railroads were built in the West, travel became faster and easier for the settlers. But for the American Indians, especially the tribes living in the Great Plains, the railroads spelled the end to a vital part of their existence.

The Great Plains, the area between the Mississippi River and the Rocky Mountains, was home to many American Indian tribes including the Blackfoot, Sioux, Cheyenne, and Arapaho. The survival of many of the tribes depended on one thing—the buffalo

*Buffalo hunts provided Plains Indians with their food, clothing, and shelter.*

At one time as many as 30 million buffalo roamed the Great Plains. By the end of the 1800s the number was less than 1,000. For the Plains Indians, the buffalo was their primary source of food and clothing. They used every part of a buffalo, leaving nothing to waste. They ate the buffalo meat and used buffalo hides to make teepees and for trade. Female buffalo hides were especially popular, and Indians traded them with white men for guns and knives.

In addition to American Indian hunters, professional hunters came through the plains, killing as many as 1 million buffalo each year. During the construction of the transcontinental railroad in the 1860s, hunters killed thousands of buffalo while clearing the land,

*Hunters shot the buffalo from trains, hunting them nearly to extinction.*

often leaving behind the bodies of the buffalo to rot in the sun. After the railroad was completed in 1869, it became easier for the hunters to send hides back East, and the number of buffalo killed increased.

## THE DAKOTA CONFLICT

In summer 1862 many Dakota Sioux Indians living on a small reservation in southern Minnesota were starving. Their crops the previous year had failed, and land payments owed them by the government had been delayed. The settlers in the area were unwilling to help them. Trader Andrew Myrick, when asked by Dakota Chief Little Crow for help, replied, "If they are hungry, let them eat grass or their own dung."

Angered, the Dakota attacked. Four young Dakota men killed five people on a farm August 18. Two weeks later Myrick was found murdered, his mouth filled with grass. The Dakota killed hundreds of settlers and soldiers during the next few weeks and burned much of the town of New Ulm. About 60 Dakota are believed to have been killed. When the conflict ended, 307 Dakota were sentenced to death, but President Abraham Lincoln reduced the number to 39. One man's sentence was commuted later. On December 26, 1862, the 38 men were hanged in Mankato, Minnesota, the largest mass execution in U.S. history.

The Dakota people's problems continued after the execution. The government took their reservation land and forced them to leave Minnesota.

*Mankato, Minnesota, was the site of the mass hanging of 38 Dakota men.*

## SHELTER AND THE GREAT PLAINS

American Indians who lived on the Great Plains adapted to the largely treeless area by living in tepees. The cone-shaped tepees were made of buffalo skins stretched over a pole framework. Tepees were approximately 15 feet (4.6 meters) in diameter. Since tepees could be easily moved from one spot to another, the Indians were able to follow the herds of buffalo and other game such as deer, elk, and antelope on the Great Plains.

## GOLD IN THE BLACK HILLS

The Black Hills of present-day South Dakota were considered sacred to the Lakota Sioux who lived there. A government treaty set aside the land for the Lakota, but when gold was discovered in the Black Hills in 1875, the government wanted to break the treaty. The government planned to force the Lakota to leave the Black Hills and move to a reservation. The Lakota refused to go.

On the afternoon of June 25, 1876, Army General George Custer and the Seventh Cavalry attacked Lakota Chief Sitting Bull's camp near the Little Bighorn River in Montana. The Lakota warriors learned of Custer's plan and launched a counterattack. The Lakota warriors numbered at least 1,500, compared to about 200 soldiers under Custer's command. Within an hour Custer was dead, along with all of his men. Although the Indians won the Battle of

*The victory at the Little Bighorn didn't allow the Lakota people to keep their land.*

the Little Bighorn, it wasn't a lasting victory. After the battle they were forced to leave the Black Hills and move to reservations—the very fate they had fought to avoid.

## THE GHOST DANCE

One nonviolent way the American Indians fought back was to dance the Ghost Dance. Part of a religious movement that swept the West, the Ghost Dance promised American Indians that the land would return to the way it used to be. It promised that great herds of buffalo would return to the land and that the American Indians would be able to return to their old ways.

*The Ghost Dance was part of some American Indian religions.*

People who participated in the Ghost Dance danced in circles while chanting and praying, all in a trancelike state. The Ghost Dance frightened people who didn't understand it. The dance led to one of the bloodiest battles between the American Indians and the U.S. government.

In December 1890 the government banned the Ghost Dance on Indian reservations, but it continued at the Pine Ridge reservation in South Dakota. The Lakota ghost dancers sent word to Chief Sitting Bull at the Standing Rock reservation in North Dakota to join them. On December 15 reservation police attempted to arrest Sitting Bull. He was killed during the fighting that followed, along with seven of his supporters and six police officers.

Once the Lakota at Pine Ridge learned of Sitting Bull's death, many of them fled the reservation. Members of the U.S. Seventh Cavalry found the Indians and ordered them to move their camp to Wounded Knee Creek. On December 29 soldiers demanded that the Indians in the camp turn over their guns. A deaf Indian man resisted, and in a violent battle, at least 150 Lakota, many of them women and children, and 25 U.S. soldiers were killed. The Indians called the incident the Massacre at Wounded Knee. It was to be the last major confrontation between Indians and whites.

*Bodies of Lakota people killed at Wounded Knee lay in the snow.*

# A CH 4 CHANGED WORLD

By 1890 the United States was a country that stretched from the Atlantic Coast to the Pacific Coast. The government's goal had been reached—white Americans had settled the West. But what did that mean for the American Indians? For most it meant life changed drastically for the worse.

After the West was settled, most American Indians had been moved from their native lands to reservations, often in other parts of the country. They didn't want to leave their homes, but had little say in what happened to them.

*Poverty levels were high and remain so at the Pine Ridge reservation in South Dakota.*

The Indians faced a difficult adjustment on the reservations.
Poverty levels were high and living conditions were poor. It was
easy for many Indians to become depressed in their new homes.
Some turned to alcohol as a way to cope with their unhappiness.
Many Indians also lost confidence in the power of their traditional
belief systems.

## CHILDREN'S HARDSHIP

The U.S. government wanted American Indians to live the same
way that white Americans did. One way was to require all American
Indian children to go to school.

*Indian children were forced to attend boarding schools, including one in Pennsylvania.*

Some American Indians students went to schools on their reservations. Others were sent to boarding schools, sometimes hundreds of miles away from their homes. The students were required to speak only English at their new schools instead of their native language. They also had to change their names to ones that sounded "American" and wear the same kind of clothes that American students did. Student Luther Standing Bear observed: "It did not occur to me at the time that I was going away to learn the ways of the white man. My idea was that I was leaving the reservation and going to stay away long enough to do some brave deed, and then come home again alive."

Most American Indian students didn't like the new ways that were forced upon them. It was hard to be away from their parents

in a new and strange environment. Punishment could be severe at the schools, and teachers and other people in authority sometimes physically or sexually abused the students.

Adult Indians were also expected to make changes in how they lived their lives. The government wanted Indians to become more like the settlers, farming the land and attending Christian churches. It didn't seem to matter what the Indians wanted. In addition to losing the land they had lived on, American Indians were losing their culture and traditional ways too. The West had been settled the way the U.S. government had wanted, but American Indians' lives were unsettled—and often lost—in the process.

## AMERICAN INDIAN SPIRITUALITY

There are many religious beliefs among the various tribes of American Indians. But a common belief shared by most was that American Indians were chosen to exist by their creator. Most American Indians respected other peoples' religious beliefs. Most also believed that all forms of life depended on each other.

White settlers hoped to introduce Indians to Christianity and brought missionaries with them. But Indians sometimes had difficulty separating how Christians preached and how they behaved, since the two could be very different. Sauk leader Black Hawk said: "The whites may do bad all their lives, and then, if they are sorry for it when about to die, all is well? But with us it is different: we must continue throughout our lives to do what we conceive to be good."

# INDEX

army, U.S., 4–5, 14, 15, 16–17, 21, 22–23, 25

battles
    Dakota Conflict, 20–21
    Little Bighorn, 22–23
    Seminole Wars, 14
    Wounded Knee, 25
buffalo, 6, 18–20, 22, 23

Clark, William, 8, 9
culture, 6, 12–13, 23–24, 29
Custer, George, 22

diseases, 14, 16

Five Civilized Tribes, 12–15

Ghost Dance, 23–24
Great Plains, 16, 18–19, 22

Hin-mah-too-yah-lat-kekt, Chief. *See* Joseph, Chief

Indian Removal Act, 13–14

Jackson, Andrew, 13, 14
Jefferson, Thomas, 8
Joseph, Chief, 4–6

land, respect for, 6, 22
languages, 6, 16, 28
Lewis, Meriwether, 8, 9
Little Crow, Chief, 20
Louisiana Purchase, 8

Manifest Destiny, 16
missionaries, 14, 29
Myrick, Andrew, 20–21

Plymouth Colony, 7

Powhatan, Chief, 6–7

railroads, 18, 19–20
Rendezvous, 11
reservations, 4, 8, 20, 21, 22, 23, 24–25, 26–28

Sacagawea, 9
schools, 27–29
settlers
    helping, 6–7, 9, 11
    conflicts with, 4, 7–8, 9–10, 16–17, 20–21
Sitting Bull, Chief, 22, 24–25
spirituality, 6, 23–24, 29
Squanto, 7

tepees, 22
Tisquantam. *See* Squanto
Trail of Tears, 14–15
trappers, 11
treaties, 8–10, 13–14, 22
tribes
    Arapaho, 18
    Blackfoot, 18
    Cherokee, 12–15
    Cheyenne, 16, 18
    Chickasaw, 12–13, 14
    Choctaw, 12–13, 14
    Creek, 12–13, 14
    Dakota, 20–21
    Lakota, 16, 22–23, 24–25
    Mandan, 16
    Nez Percé, 4–6
    Patuxet, 7
    Seminole, 12–13, 14
    Shoshone, 9
    Sioux, 18, 20, 22

Wahunsenacawh, Chief. *See* Powhatan, Chief

# GLOSSARY

**CANNIBALISM** —the eating of human flesh by another human being

**CHOLERA** —a deadly disease that causes vomiting, diarrhea, and dehydration

**DESTINY** —predetermined course of events

**HOMESTEAD** —a piece of land given to a settler by the U.S. government for a new home and farm

**IMMIGRANT** —someone who moves from one country to live permanently in another country

**IMMUNITY** —the ability of the body to resist disease

**MASSACRE** —the needless killing of a group of helpless people

**RENDEZVOUS** —a French word meaning a prearranged meeting; a meeting of trappers and American Indians during the 1800s

**RESERVATION** —an area of land set aside by the U.S. government for American Indians

**TREATY** —a formal agreement between groups or nations

# INTERNET SITES

Use FactHound to find Internet sites related to this book. All of the sites on FactHound have been researched by our staff.

Here's all you do:

Visit *www.facthound.com*

Type in this code: 9780756545710

# TIMELINE

## 1763

In a treaty that ends the French and Indian War, France gives up Canada and the land in the Ohio Valley to England and its land west of the Mississippi River to Spain

## 1783

The United States wins the Revolutionary War with Great Britain and gains all the land from the Great Lakes to the Gulf of Mexico and all the land from the Appalachian Mountains to the Mississippi River

## 1787

Congress passes the Northwest Ordinance, establishing government and laws in the area north of the Ohio River and east of the Mississippi River

## 1800

France regains the North American land it ceded to Spain after the French and Indian War

## 1840

Settlers began traveling west on the Oregon Trail

## 1845

The U.S. annexes the Republic of Texas

## 1848

The Gold Rush begins; the United States adds what would become the states of California, New Mexico, and Arizona after winning the Mexican War

## 1858

The last of the three Seminole Wars ends

## 1862

The Homestead Act offers settlers free land in the West

## 1803

The U.S. buys 828,000 square miles (2.1 million square km) of land from France in the Louisiana Purchase

## 1804

Meriwether Lewis and William Clark take a group of explorers west to look for a water route to the Pacific Ocean

## 1830

Congress passes the Indian Removal Act, making Indian removal the official U.S. government policy

## 1838

Cherokee Indians are forced to move from Georgia to Indian Territory; their journey becomes known as the Trail of Tears

## 1863

Construction of the transcontinental railroad begins in California and Nebraska

## 1869

The transcontinental railroad is completed in Promontory, Utah

## 1876

General George Custer and about 200 of his soldiers are killed during the Battle of the Little Bighorn

## 1890

The Ghost Dance leads to the Battle of Wounded Knee in South Dakota; the U.S. Census Bureau announces that there is no longer a clear Western frontier line

# SELECT BIBLIOGRAPHY

Appleby, Joyce, et al. *The American Journey.* Columbus, Ohio: McGraw-Hill, 2012

Boyer, Paul S. *Holt's American Nation.* Austin, Texas: Holt, Rinehart and Winston, 2005.

Linder, Douglas. The Dakota Conflict Trials of 1862. 12 April 2012. http://law2.umkc.edu/faculty/projects/ftrials/dakota/dak_chrono.html.

Indian Removal. 8 March 2012. www.pbs.org/wgbh/aia/part4/4p2959.html

Pendergast, Tom, and Sara Pendergast. *Westward Expansion: Almanac.* Detroit: U X L, 2000.

Schissel, Lillian, ed. *Women's Diaries of the Westward Journey.* New York: Schocken Books, 1982.

Timeline of Events in Westward Expansion. 12 April 2012. www.bookrags.com/history/timeline-of-events-in-westward-expa-werl-01

Transcontinental Railroad. American Experience. 12 April 2012. www.pbs.org/wgbh/amex/tcrr/sfeature/sf_interview.html

Utley, Robert, and Wilcomb E. Washburn. *The American Heritage History of the Indian Wars.* New York: American Heritage Publishing, 1977.

Western Indian Wars. 12 April 2012. www://americanhistory.si.edu/militaryhistory/printable/section.asp?id=6

Woodworth, Steven E. *Manifest Destinies: America's Westward Expansion and the Road to the Civil War.* New York: Alfred A. Knopf, 2010.

# FURTHER READING

Berne, Emma Carlson. *Sacagawea: Crossing the Continent with Lewis and Clark.* New York: Sterling, 2010.

Bjornlund, Lydia D. *The Trail of Tears: The Relocation of the Cherokee Nation.* Detroit: Lucent Books, 2010.

Haugen, Brenda. *Crazy Horse: Sioux Warrior.* Minneapolis: Compass Point Books, 2006.

McNeese, Tim. *The Oregon Trail: Pathway to the West.* New York: Chelsea House Publishers, 2009.